SOMERSET

by

HILARY BINDING

COUNTRYSIDE BOOKS

NEWBURY · BERKSHIRE

COUNTRYSIDE BOOKS
3 Catherine Road
Newbury, Berkshire

ISBN 1 85306 592 7

Produced through MRM Associates Ltd., Reading
Typeset by Techniset Typesetters, Merseyside
Printed by Woolnough Bookbinding Ltd., Irthlingborough

CONTENTS

The author outside the privies, plumbed in the late 1880s, behind her house in Carhampton. (Courtesy of the *Western Daily Press*)

FOREWORD

On starting to research this book, it very soon became clear to me that the outdoor closet, or privy, is something that most people look back on with affection. However glad people may have been to welcome in the modern loo, for those who used it the old privy was a way of life and was taken for granted just as the indoor flush toilet is today.

When the news got out that I was writing a book on Somerset privies the letters poured in and the telephone never stopped ringing. Everybody seemed to enjoy telling me their memories and their funny stories which in some cases were still making them laugh sixty or seventy years after the event. Several older people said how glad they were to recall the old days and to be able to share them with me. I certainly have enjoyed reading every letter and all the conversations that I have had.

Then there were those who got in touch to tell me that they had a privy or knew of one somewhere. There are an amazing number of them about in Somerset and each one seems to be owned by a person eager to show it off even if it is now slightly the worse for wear. I must just mention here that all the privies described and photographed in this book are on private property – please can I ask you to respect that privacy.

These days we take our modern conveniences for granted so I was glad to hear from Brian Turner, administrator of the charity Project Romania, based in Chard. The project works with six Romanian villages, none of which has mains water or sewage schemes, and Brian told me how it is a major cultural shock for visiting westerners, used to their home comforts, to have to make use of the privies they encounter there. Memorable occasions have been finding a dead chicken down the hole; hearing a strange noise which turned out to be a pig snuffling round the outlet and being peered at up the same hole by giggly children.

If you compare these stories with those in this book you will realise that the situation is not much different from that of rural Somerset not so very long ago.

Only yesterday I was told of a former privy over a pond where one day, as the rather large farmer's wife lowered herself onto the well-worn seat, it gave way and she toppled in. Not funny for her, but it makes me smile just to write it down. So, smile with me at the memories recorded here – but let this book also be a salutary reminder of how lucky we now are.

HILARY BINDING

[1]

PRIVIES PAST

The history of the privy is shrouded not only in the mists of time but in a miasma of euphemisms. Certainly from the medieval period onward it seems that people used any expression to avoid saying that the moment had come to go and carry out a simple and universal bodily function. And so they would visit the necessary house, the garderobe (wardrobe!), the place of easement, and would later talk of going to spend a penny, see George or a man about a dog, powder their nose and so on. There is a coyness about all this which hardly matches the basic provision which existed in this country for many people right up until the 1950s. The whole situation seems to be summed up by a tongue-in-cheek remark, 'We have nothing vulgar in the *Victoria County History*', made to me by the editor of that erudite survey of Somerset's history. The Victorians are said to have swathed the legs of their tables with cloths because it was considered indecent to 'show a leg' so one would hardly expect them to talk about privies. Yet it was the Victorian period that saw sanitary conditions in towns so appalling that they could only be compared with those of medieval London and, as a consequence, provided an impetus for the greatest advances in the development of sanitation.

When the Romans came to this country they must have been shocked at our total lack of plumbing since their own water supplies, bathing systems and latrines were highly organised both for civilians and for the military. At Housesteads on Hadrian's Wall an elaborate system included a suite of bathrooms for the barrack blocks where surplus water flushed the latrines and a tap provided for an occasional more thorough flush. Along the two

A Roman military communal latrine, with running water both beneath and in front of the sitters and sponge wiping sticks in a central bowl.

sides of the 31 ft long latrine can be seen channels over which would have been wooden seats with holes. Doubtless a similar system was installed at military centres in Somerset such as Charterhouse though no latrine pits have been found there.

When the Romans left they took with them all their ideas about sanitation and people reverted to using holes in the ground. Not that many of the British would have done anything else even while the Romans were in occupation. It was the monks who were to set a new civilising standard. They sited their monasteries near rivers and streams, installed water supply and drainage systems, and latrine blocks known as reredorters were built with facilities upstairs for use at night. At Cleeve Abbey a stone doorpost in the corner of the dormitory marks where a door led into the upper gong or latrine. Beside the post is a hook to hold a lamp that would burn all night to light the way. Although the reredorter no longer exists the stone-built drainage system is evident. Downstairs a laver provided washing facilities and nearby there may have been closets. At Muchelney Abbey the lower storey of the thatched reredorter may originally have been used for storage. Upstairs wooden seats with holes would have been placed over the chutes which were built into the walls. There may have been individual cubicles. At Glastonbury the latrines were built above a channel bringing water from Chalice Well to the Gatehouse.

In castles and other important houses there were internal privies known as garderobes. These were usually built within the thickness of the walls, each with a vertical shaft below a stone or wooden seat or, alternatively, in a separate tower. If there was no stream or moat the waste would fall to a large pit or cellar which then had to be cleaned out by people known as gong-fermors (gong from the Saxon 'gang', to go off, and fermor from the Saxon 'fey', to cleanse) who certainly deserved the high rates of pay which they earned for this noisome task. Inevitably these

The thatched reredorter at Muchelney Abbey was once linked to the monks' dormitory so that the upstairs latrine was easily accessible at night.

garderobes were draughty and sometimes they were built into chimney breasts for added warmth. There were garderobes in smaller houses as well. In Carhampton a small medieval hall-house boasted a garderobe tower over a stream until the house was burnt down and rebuilt without it. In some places the garde-robe today is a mystery to its owners. At the George and Pilgrims inn in Glastonbury an L-shaped passage ending in a small bulge was thought to be a confessional though it was wondered why there was only room for one!

Garderobes had their drawbacks and many of the upper classes were concerned with improving the system in their homes. It was while visiting Sir Matthew Arundell at Wardour Castle where the guests were discussing the problems of garde-robes and close stools – rather like comfortable commodes – that Sir John Harington, wit and favourite of Elizabeth I, deter-

The Bishop's Palace at Wells showing the medieval garderobe tower (centre) built by Bishop Jocelin (1206–1242) with a window added after change of use by Bishop Bekynton (1443–1465). The tower almost certainly drained to a pit. (Pigot Collection, Somerset Archaeological and Natural History Society)

mined to invent something that would be an improvement. In 1596 he published his satirical *Metamorphosis of Ajax* (a pun on 'jakes', a common name for the privy) which contained an account of his invention for the 'common benefit of builders, housekeepers and houseowners'. The central part of the work is devoted to a careful description of a water closet which performed all the functions of a modern water closet: cleaning the pan, carrying away the water and sealing off the stench.

Sir John installed his invention at his home at Kelston, just north of Bath, and so was able to provide full details, from the cistern and water supply to the brick, stone or lead receptacle which was placed over an existing privy shaft and the techni-

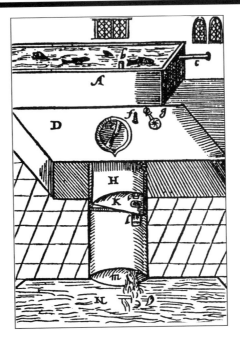

Sir John Harington's Ajax.

calities of making the water fall 'down at a gallop into the JAX'.
It is said that a water closet on Harington's model was built at
Richmond for the Queen but maybe it didn't work well! Sir John
fell out of favour, was banished from court and eventually died in
penury.

It is generally assumed that Harington's water closet was not
very satisfactory but a full-scale working model made at the
Gladstone Pottery Museum in Longton, Stoke-on-Trent under
the enthusiastic guidance of Jonathan Kinghorn proved otherwise. It worked very well, providing a real gallop of water. The
problem was that it still discharged into moat, garden or cellar
and it also needed a proper water supply which most people did

12

not have. Harington was a man some two hundred years ahead of his time.

By the early 18th century water closets of the sluice type were being used in most big houses. At Windsor, Queen Anne had installed 'a little place with a seat of easement of marble with sluices of water to wash it all down.' In Somerset, at places like Clanville Manor at Castle Cary and Chilthorne Domer manor, privies were built over water systems designed to carry away the waste. By the end of the century more improvements were being made to the water closet. In 1775 Alexander Cummings took out a patent for a water closet with an S-bend 'stink trap' which prevented noxious gases seeping back into the house. Unfortunately its emptying valve did not work well but this was improved on three years later by Joseph Bramah whose firm set the standard for the next hundred years – over 6,000 had been installed by 1797 – and the word 'bramah' passed into colloquial use to describe something really first-rate.

One of the many types of water closet was the long hopper of the 1850s which was flushed from the top by a thin spiral of water with the disadvantage that 'by the time it has twirled itself down to the trap it has no energy left to carry anything with it.' Maggi Adams recalls a long hopper at their house at Combwich still in use at the beginning of the 1980s. Waste water from the house passed into a hopper which, when full, automatically flushed out the ceramic bowl.

As the 19th century moved on improvements came thick and fast but these technically-advanced water closets were not for the use of the poor. Conditions in the old towns were at their worst in Somerset in the mid-1800s (see Chapter 6) when epidemics forced Borough Councils to take action to improve matters. In the newly-developing tourist centres, however, good water supplies and sanitation were a priority and many an early hotel advertisement boasts 'perfect sanitation'.

Advertisements from sanitary plumbers snowballed towards the end of the 19th century.

One important side-issue was the earth closet invented in 1860 by the Rev Henry Moule of Fordington in Dorset following an outbreak of typhoid in the area. In its simplest form there was a wooden seat with a bucket underneath, and above it at the back a hopper filled with fine dried earth, charcoal, ashes, sand or sawdust. When a handle was pulled a layer of earth fell into the bucket which was emptied at intervals. The end-product of such a process would quickly become sterile and inoffensive.

Hotels and guesthouses were eager to announce their improved sanitary arrangements.

15

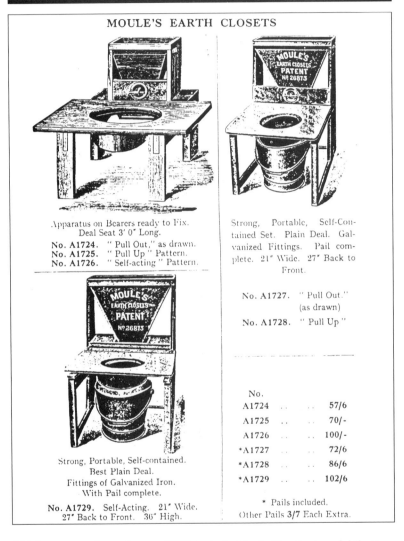

MOULE'S EARTH CLOSETS

Apparatus on Bearers ready to Fix.
Deal Seat 3' 0" Long.

No. A1724. " Pull Out," as drawn.
No. A1725. " Pull Up " Pattern.
No. A1726. " Self-acting " Pattern.

Strong, Portable, Self-Contained Set. Plain Deal. Galvanized Fittings. Pail complete. 21" Wide. 27" Back to Front.

No. A1727. " Pull Out."
(as drawn)

No. A1728. " Pull Up "

Strong, Portable, Self-contained.
Best Plain Deal.
Fittings of Galvanized Iron.
With Pail complete.

No. A1729. Self-Acting. 21" Wide.
27" Back to Front. 36" High.

No.		
A1724	.. ..	57/6
A1725	.. ..	70/-
A1726	.. ..	100/-
*A1727	.. ..	72/6
*A1728	.. ..	86/6
*A1729	.. ..	102/6

* Pails included.
Other Pails **3/7** Each Extra.

This ironmonger's catalogue of 1936 included the 'self-acting' model (bottom left) which delivered the contents of the hopper automatically when the user stood up.

Hugh Flatt near the entrance to the earth closet which he still uses in the summer. The waste is mixed with sawdust and household waste to form a wonderful black, friable compost.

One of the most interesting people whom I met as I did my research was Hugh Flatt. Now in his eighties he is an enthusiast for the earth closet both philosophically and environmentally and still uses one in the summer months. He sees the proper use of the earth closet as the natural way of recycling human waste and returning goodness to the soil.

Hugh used bucket lavatories for many years but never added chemicals. Instead he used sawdust – or sawdust mixed with soil – in their buckets, adding some each time after use, the sawdust being both absorbent and sweet-smelling. Each day the buckets were emptied. The base for the compost heap was an area of soil and it was started with a layer of cut weeds, grass or straw. The

17

contents of the bucket were covered with materials that would reduce to a minimum any unpleasant smell or direct access to flies. Suitable kitchen waste was added and every three weeks a thin layer of soil was spread over.

After three or four months Hugh would close the heap, topping it up with a good layer of green material or straw and finishing with a layer of soil. It was then left for another four months, turned once to give it a final aeration and, within another three weeks or so, fresh-smelling, friable biologically active compost was ready to spread on the garden. The compost that Hugh showed me was just like that and his vegetable garden bore witness to its use. He is well aware of the problems of using such systems in our highly-populated towns and cities but feels strongly that authorities should turn their attention to proper recycling as a way of safeguarding the earth's resources.

Certainly in the Somerset countryside similar systems were used into the 1950s and '60s which is why there are so many wonderful privies for us to visit.

[2]

PRIVY DESIGN

Once you begin to look for privies you notice old privy buildings everywhere. After all, almost every house and cottage in the last century, and many well into this century, had a privy and although some have been demolished many others have been put to good use as sheds or stores. Within about two hundred yards of where I live in Carhampton there are at least a dozen privy buildings including single ones in cottage gardens, a row in the old school playground, some behind the old Wesleyan schoolroom and a block of three down at the old tannery. They are easily recognisable, often isolated from the main building and usually with distinctive features.

Having said that, it would be quite wrong to assume that every privy building looks just like all the rest because it certainly doesn't. Single privies were usually small square or rectangular buildings and, as one correspondent pointed out, usually much larger than many of today's public lavatories where you can hardly turn round, especially if you are loaded with shopping bags! Some had pitched roofs while others had single sloped roofs which made them look as if they were lean-tos even if they weren't. The latter were the most economical design, using a minimum of building materials; one wall high enough for a door, the one opposite high enough to accommodate someone sitting down, simple rafters resting between the two and the side walls built up to reach the sloping roof.

Building materials reflected the locality. On Exmoor most privies were constructed with old red sandstone, on the Mendips grey limestone dominated and, most distinctive, the beautiful privies of Norton sub Hamdon and area were built in luscious,

19

This privy at Knapp Cottage, Wheddon Cross demonstrates economy of design. The entrance was through the higher wall and the seat faced it, so using as little stone as possible.

golden Ham stone. Those in the vicinity of Keinton Mandeville were built with Keinton Bluestone. Brick was sometimes used where there were local brickfields and was the more usual material for later privies.

A few privies were, within living memory, made of cob, that mixture of mud, dung, horse-hair and straw used in the building of many West Somerset cottages, but we did not come across any still standing. Elsie Harris remembers that her grandmother's privy at Doniford was built of cob and had a thatched roof. Roofs, too, varied depending on the building style and materials in the area. There are slate roofs on privies in the Brendons constructed with slate from the quarry at Treborough. Many in

Well-built in Ham stone, this privy at Brook House, Norton sub Hamdon once stood at the corner of the walled vegetable garden.

West Somerset, including my own, were roofed with pantiles – the lord of the manor at Dunster Castle had a brick and tile works nearby – while others in mid-Somerset boast Roman or double Roman tiles. Those in Ilchester were roofed with pantiles or Ham stone tiles. Many may once have been thatched but as the thatch wore out it was cheaper to replace the roof with corrugated iron, which made it very noisy when it was raining!

Sometimes a row of cottages would have a row of privies, one for each property. but in towns privies were often shared. Mrs Hounsell, who is now 90, wrote to tell me about the privies in Chard when she was growing up. 'My parents lived at Bath Street, Chard and brought up a family there. There was a large yard at the side of our house (No 9) but the family at No 8 had to

Corrugated iron covers many roofs of farm privies. This two-seater is at Upcott Farm, Brushford.

A row of three once serving three cottages at Norton sub Hamdon is now a garden shed.

Another row of three at Brompton Regis, now used for garden storage.

go out of their front door to get to the yard and toilet. It was shared by both families and at one time there were thirteen people using it. There was no flush, just a wooden seat boxed in. We had to carry pails of water to flush it.' In Crowshute Gardens, Chard the privy was housed in a wooden shed, was shared by two families and, again, flushed by hand.

Some privies were built back to back which allowed some scope for extra-mural activities. Mrs Ashley, who now lives at Charlton Horethorne, remembers that as a girl she and a friend would wait for their elderly neighbour to get settled on his side and then would poke a stick through a crack in the wall. 'Needless to say he was extremely annoyed. We would give him a break and let him think it wouldn't happen again but it did until we were found out!' Mr Clark of Bristol remembers being able to talk to his friend, Bert, through the wall.

Mrs Ashley recalls that they once had a wooden hut in the garden as a privy. 'Known as the sentry box, it was far enough away from the house for the children to demand an escort when it was dark.'

Some farms had two separate privies, one for the family and one for the farm workers. Ken Parsons remembered that there were two at Grange Farm, Hutton when he was young. At West Harwood Farm near Cutcombe there were two three-seaters while at Manley Farm, Nynehead the privies were back to back; the one facing the house was for the family and the other, facing the yard, for the men.

Privy doors have all too often been replaced but we know that usually there was an opening at the top to let in air and light. Occasionally there was a small window or slit in the wall, designed not so much for the user to see out but for others to see whether anyone was in situ. Often the door was hung six inches or so above the ground so that you could see if there was a pair of feet in view. If so you knew it was 'engaged'. This could occa-

There was a good sized window in the wall at Kelsons, Wedmore.

sionally turn to a person's disadvantage if they were hoping to hide in the privy undetected. Mr Meecham's family ran a travelling shop in the Crewkerne area for more than sixty years. The van with paraffin tank and goods inside was hung about outside with pots and pans and brushes to supply the villagers. Once, just before the Second World War, Mr Meecham's father had a customer who was not a very good weekly payer. On knocking on the cottage door to collect the money he would sometimes be answered by a school lad who would say, 'Mother is not in.' One day Mr Meecham's father looked up the garden path and saw just where Mother was. 'Next time Mother goes to the lavatory,' he said to the boy, 'tell her to keep her feet up.'

Inside the privy, usually opposite the door, was the 'sanitary throne'. This was constructed of plain wood, often elm but sometimes oak. Many privies had seats of different heights (about twelve inches for children and eighteen and a half for adults) to accommodate all members of the family comfortably. The round holes cut in the wood were also of different sizes to cater for, as J. Stevens Cox wrote in 1982, 'the bums of youth and age'. When Mr Stevens Cox conducted a survey of the privies remaining in Ilchester he had drawings made of all the permutations of seats that he found. These ranged from one to four holes: one adult, one child; two adults, one child; one adult, two children and two adults, two children. One assumes that these wooden constructions were altered to suit the different demands of families as children were born, grew up and moved away. You can never predict what you will find behind a privy door. At Gudenham Manor near Wellington there was a three-holer with three different sized holes and occasionally one finds that the holes are elliptical rather than round.

Holes were often covered with 'plugs' with handles as well as a wooden lid. There was always a real danger that a child could fall through the bigger holes and drown or suffocate.

This charming indoor privy is usually referred to as a 'mother and daughter'.

You would think that with such a choice of holes all would be satisfied, but no. I am told that one critic complained:

> 'This round house is no good at all,
> The seat's too high and the hole too small.'

What reply could there be but:

> 'You leave yourself open to the obvious retort,
> Your arse is too big and your legs too short.'

Two-seaters at, top: Bay Tree Cottage, Stogumber; bottom: Kelsons, Wedmore; top opposite: a three-seater at Stoughton Cross House.

While many privies were constructed over water or an open earth pit, those in Ilchester had their seats positioned over brick or lias-stone rectangular pits some four feet deep below ground level. They were all very draughty. I have peered down several holes to examine what lay beneath and the wind has whistled in my face.

In the later years of the 19th century, though before the self-flushing water closet became common, ceramic bowls were sometimes inserted under the wooden seat. These had to be flushed by hand and, if not looked after carefully, were not always the hygienic advance that they might appear to have been. Privy floors, however, could be scrubbed regularly, being stone-flagged, tiled or built from bricks.

Occasionally privies could be very makeshift. Mrs Wiltshire from Gloucestershire wrote to tell me of the times when she stayed with an old aunt on Minehead sea front not far from the golf course. 'My aunt married when she was 60 years of age and

29

These ceramic bowls at Hill Farm, Wraxall would have been underneath the wooden seat. They were flushed by hand into a soakaway.

lived with my Uncle George in a corrugated hut that he had built. As time went by he enlarged the property by adding small corrugated iron rooms to the building. The worst thing was sleeping in the middle of the building for there was no window in the room and I used to be very frightened. There was a chemical toilet at the bottom of the garden, a huge tin drum with a wooden seat perched on top in a corrugated tin hut that I remember as being awful. It was always full up to the brim with newspaper and was so high that I never wanted to sit on the seat. It was smelly and a discouraging place to visit, enjoyed mostly by flies and spiders. Either a chemical or some lime was dropped in regularly to try to keep things decent.'

Does this corbel above the unusual window indicate a great age for this privy at Manor Farm, Norton sub Hamdon?

This privy houses a water closet system dated 1900. The building suggests that before that date it was a 'bucket and chuck it' privy. The roof would not have been thatched originally.

It is not easy to tell the age of a privy from its design, which depends more on the area and the status of the family property than on age. Crude design does not necessarily mean that the building is old though it may be so. Equally, some of the best built privies are extremely old. The handsome six-seater at Chilthorne Domer is thought to be 18th century or earlier and many farm privies may also be of that age or older. That at Clanville Manor, set in the corner of the brick walled vegetable garden, was probably built at the same time as the house, 1743. The medieval Hill Farm at Wraxall was rebuilt in 1671 and it is thought that the privy is contemporary.

Scarce historical evidence tells us the age of a few others. A row of cottages was built by the Luttrell family in 1750, to house farm and forestry workers at Woodcombe, Minehead. Each was provided with a brick-built privy, a pig sty and a long garden. Certain privies we know were built in the mid-19th century as people came to understand more about the links between sewage, water supply and disease and more attention was paid to the need for hygiene. Good rural landlords like Berkely Napier, of East Pennard, and Sir Alexander Hood, of Fairfield, Stogursey, built new cottages for their labourers with privies. Sir Alexander's included back to back privies built at the far end of the wall dividing the gardens of semi-detached cottages, with cesspools that opened with a stone trap. Those on the Napier property had privies built onto the back of the house, with the kitchen window opening at right angles to the privy door. The Prince of Wales' model cottages at Isle Brewers also had privies built on the back of the house while, at Clevedon, Sir Arthur Elton's new cottages had privies actually in the building. These are all noted in Mr Boyle's evidence presented to the Commission enquiring into the working conditions of women and children in agriculture, 1867. Mr Boyle did not like the idea of privies being so close to the house but he notes that the occupiers all

Brick privies built at Woodcombe, Minehead around 1750. They were built by the Luttrells of Dunster Castle with brick from their own kilns.

say that there is no smell. They were probably glad not to have to trek down the garden.

In the 1870s on the Holnicote estate near Porlock Sir Thomas Dyke Acland, the eleventh baronet, was spending money on cottage improvements. In a letter to his brother Henry dated 3 October 1874, he wrote, 'The cost annually in repairs and small improvements [to the cottages] about £400 – they cost my father this; I paid that sum the first year in porches, better windows, privies etc., and some thatching.' Several of these privies are still in existence and are likely to remain so as they are now in the care of the National Trust which today owns the estate.

Back to back privies and stores at Allerford, Minehead. These were built by
Sir Thomas Dyke Acland, eleventh baronet, in the 1870s.

Most of Somerset's towns were, and still are, small rural market
towns and ports and apart from the few big centres, Bridgwater,
Frome, Taunton and Yeovil, privy arrangements were similar to
those in the country. J. Stevens Cox discovered that most of the
privies he found in Ilchester were sited ten to thirty or more feet
from the house, although a few directly adjoined the house but
always with a door facing to the garden. Some were at the
bottom of the garden. In the coal mining area of North Somerset
many new houses were built in the late 19th century, often in
terraced rows and here each house or pair of houses had its own
privy. They were sometimes built back to back so that you could,
if you wished, communicate with the occupant next door.

Many privies in rural towns and villages were in use up until the early 1960s but even when the new systems arrived all was not necessarily sweetness and light. Over at Clanville Manor in 1946 Harry married Peggy, a nurse from London used to running water and proper sanitation. There was a pump outside and a privy down the garden. Although water was available in the milking parlour it was a year before a bathroom was installed at the farm and another three or four months before water was piped to the house. Water had to be collected from the dairy, brought to the house, boiled in an old copper in the back kitchen and carried up to the bathroom. The outdoor privy continued in use for many years.

At that time many farms had both outdoor privies and theoretical indoor lavatories. One, halfway up the stairs at Hutton was referred to as 'topbottom of stairs'. These indoor privies were often flushed by a limited system, perhaps rainwater collected in a tank in the roof or water pumped up by hand. Whatever the case, the indiscriminate use of indoor lavatories was often discouraged save at night or in cases of illness.

[3]

DOWN THE STAIRS AND
OUT THE BACK

'The chamber pot under the bed was not a fashion, it was a necessity. In the East Somerset farmhouse of my childhood, the lavatory was a long way from the bedroom. Down the backstairs, along a dark passageway, through the boiler house and through into the garden.' So writes Jean Pilgrim, and her experience of those days is typical.

In this rural county of Somerset privies were situated, when possible, as we have seen, well away from the house, perhaps at the end of the garden or in an orchard, and often on ground sloping away from the house and the domestic water supply to avoid both smells and contamination from soakaways. This inevitably entailed a walk of anything from ten to thirty yards, sometimes navigating buildings and avoiding muckheaps on the way. One ninety-year-old recalls that to reach the privy from their farmhouse near Chard you had 'to cross the yard, go through a shed where the milk was kept in churns overnight, and go a bit further on round the corner.' At Doniford near Watchet the privy was at the end of an avenue of apple trees, just past the hen-house. Some privies were in a small complex of buildings which included pigsties and rooms for storage.

For many youngsters the regular evening 'down the garden' visit to the privy in winter was a real nightmare. It was quite dark, no friendly street lights lightened the gloom, and there were scary noises and waving shadows. Jill Rice from Compton Dando remembers a huge walnut tree near the entrance to their privy which loured and threatened. Frequently younger children would wait for their older brothers and sisters and go

A privy at Newton St Loe near Bath made of Mendip limestone. Note the gap at the top of the door which let in light.

together to the little house. Even grown-ups would accompany each other on this last event of the day and, if the accommodation allowed, would sit companionably discussing the day's affairs. Others, perhaps with privies shared between families, preferred to wait until there was nobody about before setting off on the 'midnight patrol'.

One person told me that they didn't carry a light to reach their privy when it was dark – they knew the route so well that they just ran – but most people carried a candle, a box of matches or a hurricane lantern to light their way down the path. Candles and lanterns were kept to hand near the back door of the house where the lantern was often hung on a hook. However, night-time visits were kept to a minimum, and if it was really necessary the chamber pot (or po) would be used instead.

Which reminds me. There were, until the 1950s, some cottages in crowded villages that had no facilities at all. The people who lived in them had to use a chamber pot and slop pail and each morning carried this out across the road to the stream to dispose of the contents.

The path to the privy was well-used. Sometimes it was simply beaten earth and ashes, but more often a more permanent way was laid; cobbles, small stones like gravel or, on occasion, flagstones. This would prevent the path turning into a mud patch in bad weather. The trip to the privy had, of course, to be made in all weathers. A pleasant stroll down the garden path was fine on a sunny May morning, but the same journey in pouring rain, fog or treacherous snow and ice was less memorable.

But privies were also places for quiet contemplation and Mrs Chorley from Porlock remembers with affection one at the appropriately named Windwhistle, near Broadwood. It was positioned outside the boundaries of the property and faced towards a wood, a plantation of large pine and fir trees where red squirrels bounded from branch to branch; a magical place. Many people enjoyed sitting with the door open surveying the apple blossom in the orchard or views across the countryside. One old lady in Bridgwater workhouse, Lucy Brice, was so fond of sitting quietly in the privy that it was no surprise when she died there in May 1862.

In Somerset it seems to have been the practice whenever possible to use running water to dispose of the waste, so many privies were positioned beside a water course. In fact the first privy that I was told about when I began this research appears to have been little more than a plank over a stream. I am not even sure whether there was a roof to keep out some of the weather.

Privies at Brookside, Brompton Regis, backing over the stream.

Many privies simply backed on to a stream, ditch, rhine or mill-leat which carried the effluent away, but in other places there were carefully-crafted systems which brought the water through a series of ponds, channels, culverts and sluice-gates, ensuring that the waste was carried away quickly. In 1724 an account of the 'drayns and gouts' at Halswell House at Goathurst shows a complex system of drainage at this great country house. A culvert, large enough to take a man, ran from the new cellar, passing under the flower garden and the stalls in the stables to feed into another drain that linked the kitchen pond and horse pond. A 'plate', perhaps a square of metal or wood, was set in the wall and could be opened if there was any stoppage so that mud could be removed. The survey goes on to explain that another drain or gout could be used if 'at any time

The remains of two three-holer privies at West Harwood Farm, Wheddon Cross. They were built back to back against a high garden wall over a water-course.

Leat leading to the ivy-covered privy at Knighton Farm, Withypool.

Privy at Brightworthy, Withypool, showing the leat at the outfall from the privy. The waste was washed through the leat and out onto the fields.

43

Clanville Manor, Castle Cary. The culvert from the privy passed under a wall and into a stone channel controlled by two sluice gates.

the little house in the flower garden becomes full or offensive.'

Out on Exmoor two farm holdings, Knighton and Bright-worthy, probably existed from Saxon times. Both houses were rebuilt sometime in the middle of the 19th century and water systems were carefully designed to deal with waste from the privies. At Knighton, a stone-clad channelled leat leads from the stream above the old horse pond and runs close to the rear of the privy before rejoining the main stream. At Brightworthy, half a mile away up the hill, there is a similar system. Here a channelled leat runs right under the old privy seat and then discreetly past the garden, taking any waste out to the fields to manure them. In both cases sluice gates were used to increase or divert the flow as necessary.

At Clanville Manor the privy was sited some eight feet above a culvert which ran underground from the horse pond, emerging beyond the privy into a stone channel controlled by sluices and known as the sheep dip, before continuing across the fields. At Priory Farm, Compton Dando the stream itself ran directly below the privy, bringing with it the effluent from cottages further up the hill. The stream has now been diverted but still runs freely and quickly down through the fields.

David Lock used to visit his grandparents at their farm at North-combe, Dulverton, some fifty years ago. Here there was a privy set over a stream and he, fresh from his life in Taunton with all its mod cons, and attending Huish's Grammar School, was fascinated. One day, leaning over the hole to see just how it all worked, David lost his prized school cap. How humiliating! It fell into the abyss and was then carried off by the stream, away and out of sight. The idea of explaining the loss of his cap to his schoolmasters and friends on Monday was unbearable for David. Fortunately the next day his uncle took the lad out over

This privy over the stream near Timberscombe once belonged to an inn, the Traveller's Rest. The bridge is modern but crossing the stream in the dark must always have been hazardous.

the fields where they found his cap, soiled perhaps, but otherwise unharmed.

Think of all the drinking that goes on in pubs! Down at the bottom of Draper's Way, an old packhorse route between Exford, Luckwell Bridge and Timberscombe, was the Traveller's Rest, a welcome stop for those passing through as well as for local men. The stream across the road was very handy for those just in need of a pee, but over the stream was the privy itself. It backed on to the water which once again would have carried waste matter away, but I do wonder how many people fell into the stream on their desperate way across the narrow footbridge. The system here was a soakaway into the stream and when Lorna Hay first moved there her son was delighted with the heap of black soil betwixt privy and water. 'I'm looking for treasure, Mother,' he cried.

[4]

WHERE DID IT ALL GO?

'Children took it all for granted. They didn't question where our end products all went,' as one correspondent said to me.

Hilary Minson, who now lives in Chard, recalls an eye-opening experience when she was young. In the early 1950s she was aware that her stepfather grew the most wonderful broad beans and peas. 'They were huge in size and tastier and nicer and more plentiful than any to be had at my relations or friends and I loved them, especially when my mother fried them with potatoes for breakfast. I was always extremely proud of my stepfather's skill at producing such wonderful vegetables. I was fascinated by the way that he would have two deep trenches across the garden which he always dug on the Sunday after Boxing Day. My mother always said that it was to let the ground breathe, and I never questioned this, although at that time I was just approaching my teens.

'One spring morning at around 6 am I had occasion to rush to the privy only to find the bucket gone. On rushing back down the garden path to find my mother, I saw my stepfather emptying the bucket into the trench. I suddenly realised just how we managed to have such wonderful peas and beans. This was the original organic fertiliser. How it would be explained on the labels of today's much sought-after "natural vegetables" is a mystery. But never to this day have I tasted better.'

This sounds to me like the wonderful 'bucket and chuck it' method which crops up in one form or another all over Somerset, wherever running water was not the answer to carrying the waste away and where there was a garden large enough to accommodate it. Stan Hector remembers the old bucket and

48

chuck it method where the effluent was placed around the greens to kill whitefly and blackfly and the rest dug into a trench and covered by ashes.

For many other people there was simply a soakaway which was cleared regularly through a trap door or hole in the wall, the ordure again being put to good use on the garden. Even in Chard Old Town where four families shared two privies in 1912 the Ministry of Health inspector wrote encouragingly that there was 'plenty of garden for disposal'.

This brings me to a problem that I have not yet fully solved. Back in the 19th century there were night soil men or scavengers in the big towns who cleared the privy waste and rubbish. Few people have been able to tell me of anyone coming to clear country cesspits and privies until much more recent times when septic tanks are cleared by 'the Council'. Nearly everyone I have spoken to claims that it was the man of the house who dug out the soakaway and emptied the buckets, and did it for neighbours unable to manage themselves. In only one or two places, including Glastonbury, do people recall the 'dunnie van' coming round. Often a neighbouring farmer would collect the effluent for it was a valuable product for manuring the fields. They tended to use ordinary pitchforks and other farm implements rather than the 'shittus scoop' found in other places.

But in Ilchester where the stone pits were emptied annually, a specially designed, galvanised iron scoop in the form of a half sphere, about nine inches in diameter, set on a stout seven foot long, straight handle, provided the means of removing the ordure from the pit to the garden. Another design had the bowl fixed at right angles to the handle. Names for this scoop included bog scoop, shit spoon, privy ladle, privy dipper and bog baler.

I recall a moment some years back when a lady who had come up in the world was being rather grand about helping with some village event. 'Don't come that with me, Maud,' said her plain-speaking cousin. 'I remember when your father used to empty the cesspits!' So there were people with that job although we seem to have forgotten about them.

One way of neutralising smells, preventing the spread of germs and composting the waste was by covering the matter with lime, earth, sand, soot, ashes or sawdust. This was usually done by hand but Moule's 'self-acting' earth closet made the action automatic. These systems seem to have been installed in Somerset only in grander properties. A fine working example is still in situ at Lympsham Manor (see Chapter 7) while another was installed at Lady Acland's Hut in Selworthy Woods, a Victorian summer house which once belonged to the Acland family from Holnicote, and now belongs to the National Trust. Glyn Webber told me that when he was a boy he would visit the Hut with its verandah in front and two rooms behind where the family used to picnic. At the back of the Hut was a privy with a seat raised above a bucket. At the back was a container which the estate workers kept filled with sieved earth. When the lid was put down a shot of earth covered the contents.

Eve Heseltine remembers very clearly the privy at her house where the mechanism was probably an adaptation of the Moule earth closet. It was a brick-built privy some 20 yards from the house. Inside, along the entire back wall was a shallow, flattish wooden structure with a lift-up lid which was filled with soot. The sitting area also extended the full width of the privy. The side sections were securely fixed but the centre sitting area was hinged somehow at the back. When not in use the front of the seat was higher than the back and the whole thing sloped backwards. 'When you sat down, the front went down with you and when you stood up the front went up again, this action releasing soot from the box at the back into a removable bucket on wheels below. A small door at the rear of the building enabled the full

Bucket for water for hand flushing at Weston House Farm, Weston-in-Gordano.

bucket to be wheeled away and an empty one wheeled in.' Because the seat was quite high at the front there was a step fixed to the front to help the user to reach the seat!

Sometimes there were more complex mechanisms for emptying the waste. Hector Hamer drew my attention to the pump system at Weston House Farm in Weston-in-Gordano owned by farmer Raymond Watson. Some years ago Hector had repaired the roof of the neighbouring pigsties and was so taken with the privy that he repaired that as well.

He carefully explained to me how the pump system worked. 'This privy with its early ceramic bowl was flushed by hand with a bucket of water into a stone tank just outside. When it was full the tank could be discharged into a farm cart by means of a chain pump operated by a hand wheel. The chain carries a series of discs along its length which fit nicely into the inverted U-shaped pipe. Turning the handle moves the chain endlessly through the pipe while each disc picks up slurry carrying it upwards and out through the discharge pipe straight into a waiting cart.'

Whether manuring fields or gardens one thing is clear, the resulting crops were wonderful. 'This was real organic food,' wrote many of my correspondents, although one young and present owner of a privy could hardly believe that human waste was used in this way. Once in the garden it was piled in a heap, covered with fresh earth, ashes, straw, leaves and other vegetation and left for a year before spreading on the garden to assist in the production of fine vegetable crops.

There are many tales which still delight. Stan Hector remembers that they used to bring their prize carrots down to the pub where one man bought them regularly, exclaiming 'They're all right!' He insisted on asking why the carrots were so much bigger

The pump at Weston House Farm, used for emptying the tank which held the waste. This was then taken by cart out to the fields.

and better and sweeter than those in the shops and was eventually told. He never bought them again. Walter Purchase remembered a bus driver who always stopped for one of his father's cauliflowers ... until he also learnt why they were so good! Mr James remembers that when he was a boy at Budleigh Hill all the waste was buried in a large pit on which his father grew magnificent cucumbers. 'He would put out big basketfuls for people to help themselves but never said what they had been grown on.'

When Jenny Kennen and her husband took over Chitcombe Farm at Huish Champflower from Hugh Flatt, the keen advocate of the earth closet and grower of wonderful vegetables we met in Chapter 1, she was almost scared by the size of the worms. 'I felt that had I stood still long enough in the veg patch

53

Bucket for holding sawdust at Chitcombe Farm, Huish Champflower.

Outlets for clearing the privy at Heathfield Manor Farm, Norton Fitzwarren.

the worms would pull me into the ground!'

And one last thought is that in this wool producing county, urine was alway useful for washing and fulling the cloth and in certain dye mixtures. It was certainly sold by the poor in Frome in the 19th century and probably in other places as well.

[5]

PRIVY PROPERTIES

Although most people assured me that their privy did not smell,
they still took precautions to ensure that the building was sur-
rounded with fragrant perfume. The most usual plants were
evergreen aromatics like rosemary, lavender and honeysuckle.
Nearby were planted scented flowers, jasmine, myrtle, sweet
william, and night-scented stock. Pat Gillard's grandmother
had a marshmallow bush near her privy in Luxborough, a
recognised treatment for piles. In the country few people have
memories of unpleasant odours I remember them as having a
strangely sweet smell but in the towns where the population
was more concentrated the bogs, as Mr Stevens Cox put it,
stank. You went in and out as quickly as you could and took a
deep breath. Those who could not bear it took themselves off to
the nearest country lane and used a handy ditch. It was not a
place to linger with a book and quite a contrast to the pleasant,
isolated country privies that most people recall with nostalgia.

While toilet rolls have been around for decades, they were not
bought by ordinary Somerset folk who preferred to spend their
money on better things. After all, these commercial papers may
have been more comfortable in use but they were also inferior in
strength. Mr Stevens Cox remembered a conversation he over-
heard in the 1930s when a shop assistant was recommending a
new and stronger type of toilet paper. She assured the customer
with all the vehemence of one who has suffered, that with this
roll 'your fingers won't break through.' Would that were so
today! So rather than waste money, thrifty Somerset folk read
their newspaper and then put it to another use, recycled it as we

Honeysuckle runs rampant over this possible privy at Knapp Farm, Norton sub Hamdon.

would say today, and so nothing was wasted.

But newspapers haven't been around in common usage for all that long. So what was used before? Back in the time of the Romans those organised people used a damp sponge on a short stick but since then most people have relied on that caught-out-in-the-country childhood method, strong leaves, preferably from a dock plant. Poorer people in towns would have used a wad of old rags.

However, paper was used by wealthier families back in the 18th century though what sort of paper is not clear. John Herne in London, a former governor of Bombay, wrote regularly to his brother-in-law in Crowcombe with news of world affairs, domestic matters and the health of the family. On 21 September

Newspaper still hangs on the wall though the old seat has gone at Brightworthy Farm, Withypool.

1749 he wrote, 'We have all taken physick today by generall consent, except your daughter Betty who is Paper Rubber and Attendant on the rest.' A few days later he wrote, 'Thank God we are all pretty well. Your Paper Rubber did her Duty so well that none of us have complained of sore backsides.' What paper? Why did it need rubbing?

In more recent times you used whichever newspaper came to the house however much one may have served for bottom-cleaning better than another. Many people only took a Sunday paper so the *News of the World* was always popular. Others regularly used were the *Daily Mail*, *West Somerset Free Press*, *News Chronicle* and *Evening World*. In most households it was a weekly chore, often the task of sons or daughters, to cut the newspaper into squares, make a hole in them with a skewer and thread through a piece of string. The paper was then hung on a nail in the privy. Sometimes the newspapers were just piled in the privy, perhaps on the window sill, so that you could help yourself. The great advantage of the newspaper method was that it provided something to read and Mary Paull recalls that in her autograph book is written a piece which her aunt discovered when quietly perusing the newspaper in the privy. I once answered a scholarship exam question with the name of an Irish playwright whom I had read about while in the privy.

Most families took a pride in keeping their privy spotless. It was scrubbed out at least once a week, sometimes every day, with carbolic soap, and Jeyes Fluid was put down the hole. Phyllis Porter of Spaxton remembers that each Saturday it was her job to clean the privy, scrub the seats, tiled floor and step. When Evelyn Hounsell was about nine years old she had to take her turn to scrub out the privy and her mother made a piece of sacking into a waist apron for her to wear. They had a ceramic pan which was cleaned with rags tied to the end of a stick.

Interior of privy with limewashed wall at 12 Woodcombe Cottages, Minehead. Note the tiled floor and the step for children's feet.

Mr Banwell at Kelsons, Wedmore with a pan of lime that is still kept on a high shelf in the privy.

One of a pair of recesses for paper or to stand a candle at West Harwood Farm, Wheddon Cross.

The inside walls of some privies were rendered, but each year it was common for them – rendered or not – to be given a coat of limewash or other paint. Several privies we visited showed signs of the walls having once been coloured blue which was thought to deter flies. In the Ham Hill area some walls were coloured ochre; presumably yellow stone dust was added to the limewash.

There were few other furnishings in the privy. Occasionally we found a stand or recess for a candle or lantern and a pail for carrying water for flushing. If disinfectant was kept in the privy it would be housed high on a shelf below the rafters well out of the reach of the children. Lime was sometimes thrown into the hole and this too was kept well out of reach in a metal container.

[6]

POLLUTED PRIVIES

Perhaps the earliest written complaint about privies in Somerset was that made in the late 16th century by Ralph Brase to the officials of the borough of Taunton. 'These are to give you to understand', he wrote, 'that John Weste have made a House of Office next adjoining to my house where I now dwelleth where was never any such there before which is very noisome to me for it is nexte to my bed where I do lie, there is nothing between that place and my bed but only a thin split wall wherefore I would entreat you that the place may be viewed and that there may be some order taken therein.'

I once stayed in a hotel with exactly the same problem and in the end I asked to change my room so I have great sympathy with Mr Brase. However, most problems of pollution were of a different nature and concerned disposal. The two main ways of disposing of human waste, by water or by burial in the garden, were generally fine in the country. Most people stayed remarkably healthy and there were generally fewer upset tummies about than there are today. One's body became immune to the germs and bacteria which these days would cause illness. One well, condemned as unfit for drinking in the 1950s, had been used for decades by a family remarkable for its longevity.

The situation in the towns was another matter. Bridgwater, Frome, Taunton and Yeovil were Somerset's four main manufacturing towns and in the mid-19th century conditions in all of them were horrendous.

In Frome in 1845 the privies emptied themselves into cesspools while the remainder went straight into the town drains which were really designed to remove surface water. Commis-

A shared privy at Albert Buildings, off Albert Street in Bridgwater, between the wars. (Courtesy Admiral Blake Museum)

sioners in their Second Report inquiring into the state of large Towns and Populous Districts declared: 'Most of them are emptied and the contents used for manure. Some convey the filth into drains; but this is a bad practice, except near the river, for it only spreads the nuisance over the town, and is offensive at every grate and opening.'

In Bridgwater matters were far worse. A correspondent to the *Bridgwater Times* in 1848 described several houses in the town with no access to a privy at all. Instead a heap of ashes near the houses served the purpose. In one of the West Street courts six of a row of eight houses were without a privy between them. The drain was choked up and effluent stood in stagnant pools while all ashes, slops and ordure were thrown over a broken-down gate to a garden opposite – a disgusting mass of filth which smelt offensive in the extreme. Another heap stood close to the well which provided water for these houses.

In the Union Workhouse we are told that in February 1849, 56 boys were sleeping in a room with just 17 beds where the water closet was attached without water. In one of the girls' bedrooms there were 19 children to six beds and 'in the room an enclosed recess without any pretensions to a Water Closet or a Common Privy, having its floor covered with foul Straw, on which the children had voided their excrements and which had been allowed to accumulate evidently for some time, and this even within their dormitory!'

In the worst parts of Bridgwater at the time the mortality rate was 25 per 1,000 and it is little wonder that when cholera reached the town in August 1849 it spread like wildfire carrying off 199 people. In nearby North Petherton where several people were also victims, one house had the drains from the privies higher up passing underneath a corner of the main room; the drain was open and 'its fluid contents imbue the wall and earthern floor with ordure.'

Houses in Old Taunton Road, Bridgwater between the wars, showing pairs of privies. Refuse is piled on the bank of the River Parrett. Although the privies are water closets some sewers still drained into the river (see left hand side). (Courtesy Admiral Blake Museum)

The Bridgwater authorities were laggardly. By 1874 there were a few water closets outside the houses but these were either flushed by throwing water in the pan or by a drain from the pump to the trap which produced just a trickle. The contents of most privies had still to be dug out by hand although there were a few more modern earth closets. Often the privies were built onto the back of the houses so that the walls became saturated and even the food became contaminated by the smell.

The antiquated drains and sewers all led into the River Parrett, refuse was left in heaps until sold and taken away, while the contents of cesspools were cleared and sold to neighbouring farmers as manure.

Taunton never suffered the same epidemics as Bridgwater but a report of 1849 shows a series of open ditches running through the town and courts of cramped houses where people shared privies that drained into open cesspools or into the earth, usually close to the well and pump. The scavengers' yard stood near the hospital in East Reach which itself had drains leading to an open ditch that carried the waste over to Mr Trood's manure works in the Priory fields.

There were urinals in the town which were particularly offensive on market days. In July 1865 the Inspector of Nuisances noted that because the company's water supply was turned off at about 12 noon the urinals at Castle Green had no flushing until the next morning and the stench from them was so great that frequently it was with difficulty anyone could remain in them for the purpose for which they had been installed. Especially bad was the one in the arcade, the nuisance from which was often experienced in the Guildhall while the magistrates were sitting. The Inspector was ordered to procure some disinfectant and apply the same!

In Yeovil it is said that the wells were actually used for the disposal of effluent!

In Burnham in 1849 sixty people living in the eleven houses that made up Unity Place shared one privy and it and chamber pots were emptied on to the ash heap which was only removed three or four times a year. The drains from the recently built Prews (now Kinver) Terrace went straight through the sea wall on to the beach, hardly ideal for the holiday visitors who were beginning to visit Burnham in the summer. The owner of the Clarence Hotel complained that some of his visitors left soon after arrival as they could not stand the smells.

With our current knowledge of the links between sewage, water supply and disease it is hard to comprehend the dreadful condi-

Privies set over the River Tone in Taunton, 1891, seen on the left. From a painting by Harry Frier. (S.A.N.H.S.)

tions under which some people lived little more than a hundred years ago. With rapid advances in medical knowledge the authorities came to realise that action must be taken to prevent future epidemics and give people the opportunity to live clean and decent lives. Proper piped sewage and drainage systems, a good water supply and sewage plants were gradually installed in all the towns and outdoor privies converted to self-flushing water closets.

Even so in the terraced houses in Chard as late as 1912 there were still privies with problems. At 67 Old Town two earth closets were shared between four houses. They were clean and there was plenty of garden for disposal but not far away at 49 Old Town there was a privy midden at the end of the garden in very bad repair and dirty. It was shared by three families. At 15

Crowshute Gardens there was a hand-flushed water closet which was actually sited in the house in a room used for washing and not even screened. Further down the road was a similar hand-flushed water closet in a wooden shed shared by two families. The Inspector considered it to be most insanitary. In the High Street was a property with a pail closet in the garden; the contents were not properly buried and caused a nuisance. There were three pails for four houses. 'There should be at least four WCs,' the Inspector commented.

But it wasn't just the towns. Although sanitary matters in rural areas caused fewer problems, there were exceptions. In my own village of Carhampton there was a diphtheria epidemic in the 1880s and at least one child died. Geoffrey Timewell, whose family have long been plumbers in the area, reminded me that at the time the village's water supply came from reservoirs above the village. The water was clean and sweet and the problem lay not with the water but with the sewage that seeped into it. After this outbreak of typhoid Mr Luttrell, the Lord of the Manor, laid a proper sewerage system to his properties in Carhampton. Owners of freehold properties were invited to buy into the scheme. The owner of the house in which I now live agreed to contribute and so, out at the back, there is a late Victorian flush system.

Stan Hector was brought up at North Wootton near Glastonbury and remembers that the school privies there were sited over a water leat. The soakaway had probably leaked into the well belonging to the school caretaker for years. In 1927 the caretaker's wife, his son and daughter, and two children who regularly ate their lunch at their house, all died of typhoid. The rural areas were not entirely immune.

[7]

PARTICULAR PRIVIES

I am sure that there are large numbers of old privies hidden away in Somerset villages that I haven't yet discovered – if the number that I *have* found is anything to go by. Many of those still extant are on larger properties: farms, mills, manor houses and so on. Most are in very rural areas where mains drainage and water did not arrive until the 1950s and 1960s while others survived because they continued to be used by outdoor staff during the day.

Some of those linked with the larger houses of the county are exceptional. Perhaps the most stunning architecturally is that at Lympsham Manor near Weston-super-Mare. The beautiful and elaborate early 19th-century Gothic style house was built by the Rev Joseph Adam Stephenson in 1814-15 as a parsonage-cum-manor house. There is an early lavatory in the house but in the grounds, away from the house and shrouded by popular Victorian shrubs, is a building listed as a Garden House but which is in fact a stupendous privy. The building matches the house with Gothic arches, a cross topping the gable and inside ogee-arch topped panelling, matching windows and sculptured faces in plaster ornamenting the ceiling.

The building was not simply ornamental. It was probably used by gardeners after the family gave it up. At some point later in the century an earth closet similar to that designed by Moule was installed and is still in good working order. Sand or sawdust was placed in the container at the rear and on the pull of a handle was released into the cavity.

Over towards Yeovil is the celebrated privy at Chilthorne Domer. A charming square edifice built with Ham stone and

This charming privy of Ham stone and roofed with Ham tiles at Chilthorne Manor was in use until 1939.

roofed with Ham tiles, it is a good working privy that was used until at least 1939. Children invited to the house for parties in the 1920s and 1930s remember using it. Its particular glory is that it has six seats, four large and two small, set above a culverted waterway some nine feet below. The water to flush comes from a spring higher up and, when there is torrential rain as there has been lately, the water in the privy reaches the level of the seats. This privy was probably built in the late 17th or early 18th century though there are Tudor foundations – an indication of how old some of our privies are.

Over at Bay Tree House at Churchill is a pair of privies used by the gardeners who tended the sumptuous gardens. One, used by the under gardener, has in recent years been used as a home

A Gothic-style privy – once a three-seater – still stands in splendour at a large house in North Somerset.

Privy in Gothic style at Lympsham Manor, built around 1815 by the Rev Joseph Stephenson.

Inside the six-seater at Chilthorne Domer. The opposite side corresponds to this.

Inside the head gardener's privy at Bay Tree House, Churchill, be-panelled as befitted his status. The under gardener next door had no panelling.

The wash house and privy at Lower Lodge, Fairfield, Stogursey, made of pitted volcanic rock.

for a pet goat now, sadly, deceased. Next door, where the goat's hay was stored, is that belonging to the head gardener, suitably furnished as became his status. There is panelling and a hinged lid covering a ceramic pot. It was almost certainly hand-flushed using water pumped from an underground brick-lined water chamber nearby.

Another stunning privy is that at Lower Lodge, Fairfield. Situated some thirty yards from the lodge, the building is a real utility room enclosing privy, wash house and cold store. Anne Sparkes tells me that this one-holer, situated about 30 yards from the back door of the lodge, looks more like a garden grotto than anything else, being built of a type of pitted volcanic stone. It, together with its companion at Top Lodge, was probably put up when Sir John Acland built the lodges in the late 18th century though it may have been rebuilt when changes were made in the 1830s. A single round aperture light allows people on the outside to know whether anyone is 'on the throne'.

Many of the privies I visited had been used by the occupiers for decades while others were on premises bought recently. Lots of other people wrote to tell me of their childhood memories and occasionally memories and privies matched. When they did I went off on a journey of exploration.

Keith Gibbs got in touch with me about his experiences as an evacuee and his reminiscences made me feel very close to him and his family. I too had forebears in Somerset and joined them for a while during the early 1940s. Although Keith's forebears came originally from Wedmore and central Somerset the family was, at the beginning of the Second World War, living in south Bristol. In the early 1940s they moved, as a family and with others, to the hamlet of Stoughton Cross on the Levels midway between Allerton and Wedmore.

'Life at Stoughton Cross House was a great adventure for a kid of nine or ten, getting used to jugs and washbasins, oil lamps, candles, pos, and, above all, doing the necessary down the garden. Included in the property was (and is) a derelict cottage used as a storage space and beyond this was a stone-built privy of very ample proportions with a substantial door, albeit with no lock and a small casement window minus a couple of panes.

'As there was no lock, a small red flag, possibly made from flannel drawers, on a short stick was thrust through the broken window when the apparatus was engaged and, as kids, it was a splendid game to put the flag out and shut the door on an empty bog and snigger at the subsequent discomfort of those waiting to ease themselves.'

The privy at Stoughton Cross House, recalled by ex-evacuee Keith Gibbs.

Keith recalls that the *pièce de résistance* was the seating accommodation itself: fine deal with nicely carpentered lids – two adult holes in tandem and a small 'trainer' for junior. The whole was erected over a deep stone-lined chasm with a stream running at the base and the wind whistled up through! The place became affectionately known to the evacuees as the 'breeze-hole'. Keith's great-aunt Amy who stayed with them from time to time perfected a way of 'sitting-on' which avoided the worst of the draught.

Coincidentally one evening a plumber, John Holt, rang to tell me of a privy that he had once seen at Stoughton Cross House while working there. The present owner, who now uses the building as a garden shed, kindly allowed us to photograph it.

Another wonderful coincidence concerned a privy in Chard. Evelyn Hounsell, who has shared with me so much of life in Chard eighty or so years ago, originally wrote to tell me about her parents who brought up a family at 9 Bath Street. Next to the house there was a large yard with a privy in the corner shared by their family and those at No 8. At one time thirteen people were sharing the one privy. There was no flush, just a wooden seat boxed in and they had to carry pails of water to flush it.

Evelyn remembers that the worst time was during the Second World War with the blackout when it was so dark that they carried a lighted candle in an enamel candlestick to light their way. But no lights were allowed in wartime and they had no torches so had to carry a box of matches in case the candle blew out.

She told me that most of the row of houses in Bath Street had been demolished but that hers was still standing. I visited Chard and beside Somerfield's new car park was a tiny row of four houses. There was the privy, now converted to a flush system, and the present owner was delighted to share her own memories of privies at Tatworth and Chard in earlier days.

[8]

PERSONAL STORIES FROM SOMERSET

Privies and humour seem to go together and there are lots of older Somerset folk who are still chuckling at incidents and misfortunes that occurred long, long ago.

The construction of privies over watercourses inevitably led to all kinds of goings-on. Two little boys who attended Allerford School had committed some misdemeanour or other and had had their backsides warmed by the headmaster, Old Brooksey. They determined to get their revenge. When the head was nicely ensconced in his privy they bundled up some old newspapers and, setting fire to them, floated them down the stream and under the little house. What the head said when he found his backside warmed is not recorded!

A similar story was told to me by Mr Sankey who, before the Second World War, worked in a factory where conditions were, to say the least, primitive. The lavatories were archaic. There was one long channel and six partitioned cubicles with a water cistern at one end and an outlet at the other. There was a flush every ten to fifteen minutes.

'We had some artful dodger who used to wait until some folk were sitting on the seats and when the flush came they would light a bundle of paper at the flush end and it would float fairly quickly the length of the gully thereby singeing the customers' bottoms. Quite a lot of howls of pain were heard.' It was very amusing unless you were one of the victims!

At a privy in South Petherton set over a leat, the children would tie a bunch of nettles to a stick and then creep up the

Allerford School is now a museum and one of the privies has a regular occupant.

The outlet at Allerford School privies. These privies don't run over the stream so did the naughty boys stuff the blazing newspaper up the outlet when the headmaster was in situ?

stream and attack from below. All good clean fun! At another farm the children threw bangers down the privy in the interests of scientific investigation – this also created chaos.

Privies were excellent places for getting rid of things you didn't really want. At least one 18th century Somerset parish register records the burial of an infant 'found stifled in the bog house'. At Clanville Manor near Castle Cary in the early 20th century one of the daughters of the house hated the straw hat decorated with cherries that she was expected to wear to church during the summer. She got rid of it by posting it down the privy.

The privy at Clanville Manor, Castle Cary, the only privy for the house until 1947.

Beryl Chorley tried to save from certain death a farm cat that had been stealing chicks – by dropping it down one of the holes in their privy at Withiel Florey. The cat was terrified and in the end her father and uncle had to help her rescue it. Fortunately in the commotion they forgot about the chicks and it was allowed to live.

Privies, especially those over running water, were notoriously cool and draughty so food needing to be kept cold was sometimes hung under the seat. They were a favourite spot for one farm labourer-cum-poacher who would hang his ill gotten gains in the farm's privy over a stream before taking them home for supper at the end of the day, or selling them on.

Mr Meecham, on his rounds of South Somerset with his travelling shop, remembered a man who was known to steal a hen or two occasionally. The local constable knew this and when complained to would go along to see him and have a look round. The man never got caught out because after 'necking' the hens he would hang them under the lavatory seat beside the bucket.

Some of the privies were very draughty so it was not surprising to learn that on occasion poultry and game were hung in them to keep cool. The postman used to leave the mail in one privy. Imagine his delight when at Christmas he found a large turkey hanging there, assumed it to be his Christmas box and thanked the family profusely for their generosity.

Mrs Street remembers a story told about her two aunts who had been to Bridgwater Fair and were rather late getting home. As a result their father locked them out and the only shelter available was the privy. Luckily there were lids over the round holes so they were able to make themselves comfortable. What was said the next morning is not recorded!

Elderly relatives were often the butt of children's jokes. 'Aunt Sally often came to visit and she always wore a long black dress and we kids used to hide in the garden as she would never shut the door. We used to tell our friends about her huge drawers but one day she caught us looking and put the stick about us. As we cried Mum came out, told us it was our own fault and that Aunt Sally was allowed to hit us if we ever did it again.'

Lorna Hay once lived at Northern Mill, Winsford with a privy at the bottom of the garden. When her father was no longer able to get down the garden a new tin galvanised privy was built at the back of the house. It was known as the thunderbox for every sound was magnified. When their godmother visited the children were expected to be on their best behaviour but all would go quiet at teatime when she visited the privy. In the house Mother warned the children to be quiet, at least by the time she returned, but the magnified noises left them all in a state of subdued hysteria.

Mrs Nancy Matthews, who is now 79, has always been complimented on her good complexion. Her father used to empty the bucket from their privy into a large cesspit which was emptied monthly. As a child Nancy remembers falling into the pit; she can't recall just how she was hauled out but puts her good looks down to this experience! I remember falling into the midden in the courtyard of a farm in Gloucestershire when I was very little. I was brought out and washed and dried in the warm farmhouse kitchen but I'm not sure that it has done much for my complexion!

The hazards of sitting on the throne over an earth pit were many. There was always the danger of being stung by nettles growing up through the hole and the fear of being bitten by a rat, while spiders either fascinated or terrified. Doreen Walker recalled leaving her grandmother's privy in a great hurry one day when a huge black spider dropped on her knee from the tiles above, but she did have the presence of mind to 'make herself tidy first!' She also remembered that in their privy at home there were always lots of spiders with tiny bodies and very long legs. She and her sister would keep well away from the walls because of them, 'but we were very interested to see the way they seemed to eat their own legs.'

June Henson reminded me that Somerset has been a tourist venue for centuries. Up at Slowley Farm above Rodhuish they were content with their oudoor privy and so were the guests who arrived knowing what to expect. One day June's mother received a telephone call from nearby Roadwater. They had double booked. Could she help? June's mother explained that they had no proper conveniences but they rang from Roadwater again and again and in the end she took the visitors. They had a wonderful holiday and when they left made no mention of the privy but complimented June's mother on her excellent meals.

One problem was knowing whether a privy was in use or not. People would sing or grunt to let others know they were there but this did not always work. Mrs Holford recalled their old two-seater privy and the day when she and her sister decided to use it together. Going up the steps to the garden path her sister shouted, 'I bags the big one,' whereupon a voice from inside said, 'No you don't.' Their father was in situ.

Fred Snell who is now 86 remembers an occasion when he was riding on the Mendips accompanying two ladies when they needed to use the privy. They were miles away from the nearest village or pub but Fred knew of a gamekeeper's cottage nearby in a wood. The ladies asked him to call for permission to use the privy and also asked him to inspect it. The gamekeeper's wife said it would be perfectly all right to use it but to tell them it was no use looking at it; there was no choice as she only had one. Fred took a quick look inside and noted a double-barrelled shotgun in one corner, a wire cage with ferrets and a sack of potatoes. Walking back to tell them the circumstances he found the ladies advancing on him in a great hurry and 'I forgot what I was going to say'. 'Is it all right?' they cried. 'Yes,' I said, 'but there's no lavatory paper, just the *News of the World!*'

While most people were really thankful when modern sanitation came to their homes there were a few who weren't. Mr Partridge of Hedging who used to farm at Horner told me this story. Once upon a time two bachelor brothers were living with their parents who owned their cottage but they had a stubborn father who refused to have the house modernised. There were no mod cons of any kind; not even water indoors. The time came when the sons, who worked with explosives, decided to leave home and look for work elsewhere but rather than offend their parents by living nearby they went overseas.

After a long time their mother wrote to say that at last their father had had the place modernised and eventually the boys decided to go home for a holiday. They arrived early one morning only to find that their mother had one big heartache. Father still insisted on using the privy at the end of the garden and refused to use the new indoor lavatory.

While Mother prepared her sons' favourite stew for their midday meal the lads decided that the only thing to do was to blow up the old privy with a small charge and time it to go off at mealtime when no one would be in danger. But, after the first course, Father got up and said, 'It's no good. I must go' and off he toddled. No words describe how the boys were feeling! Then, just a few moments later there was a mild thud and shortly after Father walked in unscathed. He exclaimed, 'Mother I don't know what you put in that stew but as soon as I sat down I blew the place up!'

Mrs Paull told me about her grandmother who refused to consider any modern conveniences. It was about 1953 and the family decided to take unilateral action. 'A plan was hatched. During the summer Granny was to go on holiday to Weymouth with one of my aunts, while the rest of the family (unbeknown to

A modern privy in the churchyard at Hinton St George.

Granny) set to to turn the pantry into a bathroom and toilet complete with a gas geyser to heat the water. The family dug deep to finance the project. Everyone worked like beavers to turn out the pantry (which I remember had staddlestones and trestles with wooden boards as table tops).

'By Saturday the work was complete and everyone waited in trepidation for Granny's return to see what she would think of her new mod cons. We found out in no uncertain manner. When shown the new bathroom she was so annoyed and refused to speak to any of the family for the next six weeks. She never did use the new bathroom, preferring to battle with the elements to use the old outside earth closet. She died in 1964 aged 90.'

[9]

PRIVIES TODAY

As we went about Somerset looking at privies we came to the conclusion that people who kept and were proud of their old privies were very special. Everyone welcomed us and was delighted to show us their privies whether they had used them in the past themselves or not.

While many privies have been pulled down others are maintained and put to good use. In most places they are in service as garden sheds and on our travels we became quite adept at rapidly clearing out bean sticks, mowers and flowers pots to find the all important seat. Some kind people cleared them for us, claiming that it was a good opportunity to tidy the shed. Others are used to house garden furniture and yet others are a dumping ground for all those things that might come in useful one day. In one or two places the privy is now a wood store (clearable) or a coal shed (not clearable) and some redundant privies have been turned into accommodation for family pets. Mrs Hiscock kept rabbits and guinea pigs in their old two-seater at Milborne Port some 30 years ago while more recently at Bay Tree House at Churchill the under-gardener's privy provided luxurious living for the family goat. At Brandish Street, Allerford, one privy was turned into a hen house. An ingenious sliding contraption allowed the birds to exit the building via the old traphole used for emptying the privy.

Up on the Brendon Hills are a number of houses built in the mid-19th century when iron ore was being mined in the area. Mrs Norman used to live at Seaview House which was built originally for the manager of the mines. A memorable thatched round house contained a privy over a 40 foot drop to one of the

The under gardener's privy at Bay Tree House, Churchill later housed a pet goat for several years.

mine adits. Today its hand-made bricks are being reused in the creation of a splendid garden with far-reaching views.

Keith Rice of Tintinhull has put his old privy to perhaps the most unusual use. When he first came to the property there were two back to back privies built of local stone with brick floors and divided by a brick partition. They served two cottages and had been considered to be very modern around 1900 when the old privy right down the garden was abandoned. They were, however, quite close to the house and took up a lot of room. Ken decided that he wanted a fish pond and it seemed the obvious thing to do to use the privies for this purpose and keep the water flowing so the lower part of the privy walls now enclose a raised-up pond.

This privy at Brandish Street, Allerford is now a chicken house. Note the ingenious pulley arrangement. During the day the chickens can get in and out by way of the old outlet. At night a panel is let down to block their exit.

Jenny Kennen's letter seems to sum up people's attitudes and affection for the old way. 'When my husband and I took over the tenancy of this farm in 1972, the only sanitation was an earth closet. There were in fact two, an indoor one and an out-door one. The indoor one was only to be used in times of great emergency.

'The outside loo was a very impressive set up. It had its own small cob shed and there was a "urinal only" and another bucket arrangement in the same little shed.

'The shed was situated in the kitchen garden, and along the

93

Keith Rice's 'privies pond' at Tintinhull.

path to get to it was mint, so that there was a built-in air freshening system. The doorway faced east so that on a fine summer's morning you could watch the sun rise if you left the door open. In winter though it was a different story and many's the time when we have had to brush snow off the seat.

'A large plum tree grew outside and another hazard was in autumn when the wasps would become drunk on ripe plums. They would fall onto the ground and some would find their way via the "urinal only" onto the seat where they would sting in a most embarrassing place.

'All sawdust and wood shavings would be carefully kept so that they could be used to cover the waste as it accumulated. A small child visitor commented, "The loo is all right except when you get sawdust up your bum."'

94

A PRIVY BY ANY OTHER NAME

SOME SOMERSET PSEUDONYMS

Bog
Bog-House
Breeze hole
Bucket and chuck it
Closet
Crapper
Dunnakin
Dunnery
Dunnie
Earth closet
George
Going down the garden
I'm going out the back

Jakes
Lavatory
Lavvy
Little house
Loo
Midden
Mixen
Necessary House
Penny House
Privy
Round house
Sentry box
Thunderbox

The term 'privy' is an Early Middle English word which derives from the Latin 'privatus' meaning apart or secret.

ACKNOWLEDGEMENTS

I would like to thank everybody who wrote to me so enthusiastically on the subject of privies and everyone who showed us their privies and allowed us to photograph them. Thanks too to all those people who took photographs for me. Sadly not all the photographs can be used and I am also aware that I have not yet visited every privy mentioned to me. However, I am hoping to prepare a permanent record of privies still extant in the historic county of Somerset so will get to them all in the end.

Without Ann Butcher this book might well not exist. She accompanied me on privy excursions around the county, took most of the photographs and even searched out more privies for me in her 'spare' time. Many thanks, Ann.

I would also like to thank particularly Sue Berry at the County Record Office who shared her considerable knowledge of Public Health in Somerset with me and came up with some fascinating documentary references.

Thanks, too, to Robert Croft for setting me on this trail; to Dr Robert Dunning for helping me identify important sites; to Tony Woolrich who allowed me unlimited access to his research on Water Supply in Bridgwater and Taunton; to David Bromwich, Michael McGarvie, Mike Jones and many others who answered my questions and provided information; and lastly to all my friends who allowed me to introduce the subject of privies into so many conversations!